JR. GRAPHIC FAMOUS EXPLORERS

Francisco Vásquez de Coronado

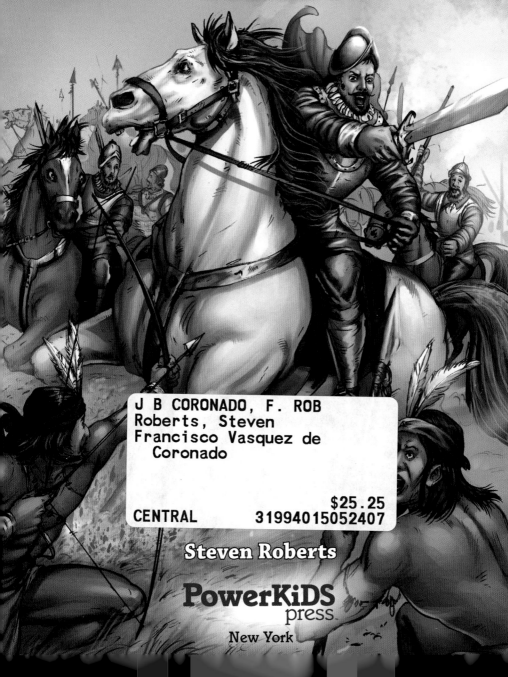

Steven Roberts

PowerKiDS press

New York

Published in 2013 by The Rosen Publishing Group, Inc.

29 East 21st Street, New York, NY 10010

First Edition

Editor: Joanne Randolph

Book Design: Planman Technologies

Illustrations: Planman Technologies

Library of Congress Cataloging-in-Publication Data

Roberts, Steven, 1955-

Francisco Vásquez de Coronado / by Steven Roberts. — 1st ed.

    p. cm. — (Jr. graphic famous explorers)

Includes index.

ISBN 978-1-4777-0070-9 (library binding) — ISBN 978-1-4777-0125-6 (pbk.) — ISBN 978-1-4777-0126-3 (6-pack)

1. Coronado, Francisco Vásquez de, 1510-1554—Juvenile literature.
2. Explorers—America—Biography—Juvenile literature. 3. Explorers—Spain—Biography—Juvenile literature. 4. America—Discovery and exploration—Spanish—Juvenile literature. 5. Southwest, New—Discovery and exploration—Spanish—Juvenile literature. I. Title.

E125.V3R64 2013

979'.01092—dc23

[B]

2012018692

Manufactured in the United States of America

CPSIA Compliance Information: Batch # W13PK1: For Further Information contact Rosen Publishing, New York, New York at 1-800-237-9932

Contents

Introduction

Francisco Vásquez de Coronado was a Spanish governor, explorer, and **conquistador**. He was the first European to explore what is now the southwestern United States, including Arizona, New Mexico, Texas, and Kansas. He set out in search of the **legendary** Seven Cities of Gold but failed to find any riches. What he did find was the Colorado River, the Grand Canyon, and the Great Plains.

Main Characters

Álvar Núñez Cabeza de Vaca (1490–c.1558) A Spanish explorer. He was one of four survivors of an earlier **expedition** and heard tales of the Seven Cities of Gold.

García López de Cárdenas (c.1540s) A member of Coronado's expedition. He was the first European to see the Grand Canyon.

Charles I, the king of Spain (1500–1558) Ruler of the Spanish Empire. He sent Coronado to New Spain to serve its **viceroy**, Antonio de Mendoza.

Francisco Vásquez de Coronado (1510–1554) A Spanish explorer. He was the first European to explore what is now the southwestern United States.

Juan Vásquez de Coronado (c.?–1532) Francisco Vásquez de Coronado's father, a wealthy nobleman.

Melchior Díaz (c.? –1541) A member of Coronado's expedition. He was the first European to see the Colorado River.

Beatriz de Estrada (1515–15??) Coronado's wife, with whom he had eight children.

Antonio de Mendoza (1495–1552) The first viceroy of New Spain. He **appointed** Coronado to search for the Seven Cities of Gold.

FRANCISCO VÁSQUEZ DE CORONADO

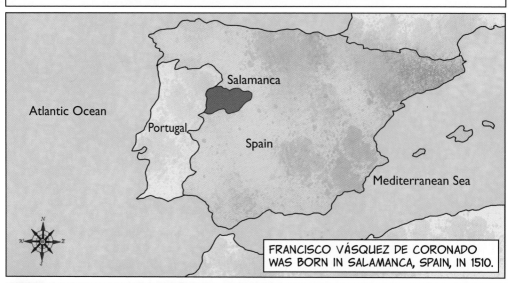

FRANCISCO VÁSQUEZ DE CORONADO WAS BORN IN SALAMANCA, SPAIN, IN 1510.

YOU WILL HAVE TO WORK. IF YOU STUDY HARD, YOU SHOULD BE ABLE TO FIND A GOOD JOB.

HE WAS THE SECOND SON OF JUAN VÁSQUEZ DE CORONADO, A WEALTHY NOBLEMAN. AS THE YOUNGER SON, FRANCISCO COULD NOT **INHERIT** THE FAMILY FORTUNE. HE WAS, HOWEVER, WELL EDUCATED.

GOOD LUCK, MY SON. MAY GOD WATCH OVER YOU.

WHEN HE WAS 25, FRANCISCO SET OUT TO SEEK HIS OWN FORTUNE.

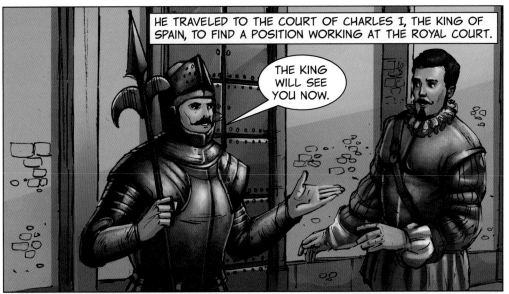

HE TRAVELED TO THE COURT OF CHARLES I, THE KING OF SPAIN, TO FIND A POSITION WORKING AT THE ROYAL COURT.

THE KING WILL SEE YOU NOW.

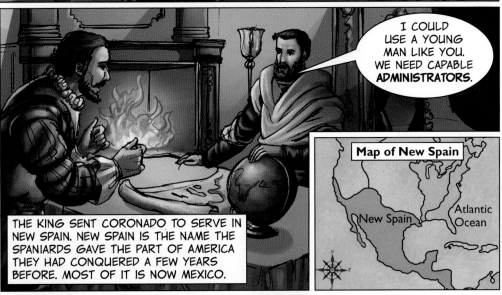

I COULD USE A YOUNG MAN LIKE YOU. WE NEED CAPABLE **ADMINISTRATORS**.

Map of New Spain

New Spain

Atlantic Ocean

THE KING SENT CORONADO TO SERVE IN NEW SPAIN. NEW SPAIN IS THE NAME THE SPANIARDS GAVE THE PART OF AMERICA THEY HAD CONQUERED A FEW YEARS BEFORE. MOST OF IT IS NOW MEXICO.

OUR FATHERS WERE FRIENDS. I WANT TO HELP YOU SETTLE IN YOUR NEW HOME.

IN 1535, CORONADO SAILED ACROSS THE ATLANTIC OCEAN TO THE NEW WORLD WITH ANTONIO DE MENDOZA, THE SPANISH VICEROY OF NEW SPAIN. CORONADO DID NOT KNOW WHAT HE WOULD FIND THERE.

MENDOZA APPOINTED CORONADO TO EXPLORE NEW LAND TO THE NORTH FOR SPAIN.

WE STILL DO NOT KNOW WHAT IS HERE. GATHER TOGETHER AN ARMY AND CLAIM THE LAND FOR SPAIN.

I WILL ALSO BRING BACK LOTS OF GOLD AND SILVER.

FORWARD, MEN! WE CLAIM THIS LAND FOR SPAIN, FOR GOD, AND FOR GLORY.

CORONADO CONQUERED THE REGION AND WAS NAMED GOVERNOR OF THE TERRITORY, WHICH WAS CALLED NUEVA GALICIA.

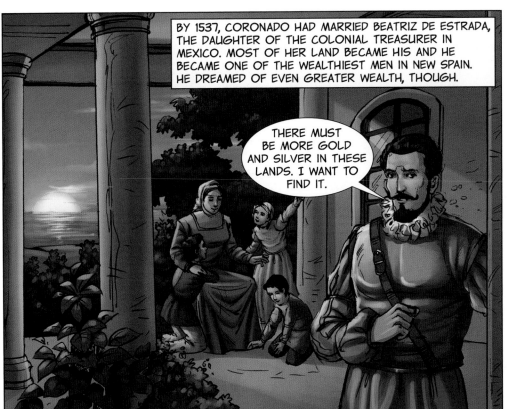

BY 1537, CORONADO HAD MARRIED BEATRIZ DE ESTRADA, THE DAUGHTER OF THE COLONIAL TREASURER IN MEXICO. MOST OF HER LAND BECAME HIS AND HE BECAME ONE OF THE WEALTHIEST MEN IN NEW SPAIN. HE DREAMED OF EVEN GREATER WEALTH, THOUGH.

THERE MUST BE MORE GOLD AND SILVER IN THESE LANDS. I WANT TO FIND IT.

THEN, ONE DAY IN 1539, A WILD-LOOKING, SUNBURNED MAN MYSTERIOUSLY APPEARED FROM THE WILDERNESS TO THE NORTH. HE DID NOT LOOK LIKE A SPANIARD AT ALL.

QUICK. RING THE BELL. WHO IS THIS WILD MAN?

THE MAN WAS ÁLVAR NÚÑEZ CABEZA DE VACA, WHO TOLD HIS STORY TO A FRANCISCAN **FRIAR**. HE WAS ONE OF FOUR SURVIVORS OF A 1528 EXPEDITION TO FLORIDA. THE OTHER MEMBERS OF THE EXPEDITION HAD DIED OF ILLNESS OR WERE KILLED BY NATIVE AMERICANS.

I HAVE SPENT THE PAST EIGHT YEARS LIVING AMONG NATIVE AMERICANS TRYING TO REACH NEW SPAIN.

CABEZA DE VACA SURVIVED BY LIVING AMONG THE NATIVE AMERICANS. DURING HIS TRAVELS, NATIVE AMERICANS TOLD HIM TALES OF A WEALTHY, GLEAMING CITY TO THE NORTH.

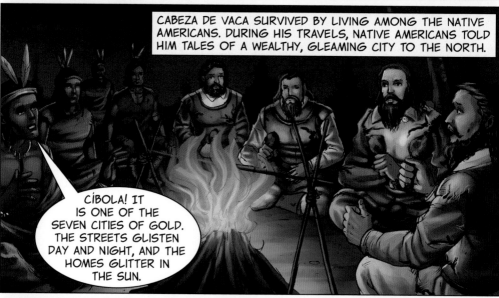

CÍBOLA! IT IS ONE OF THE SEVEN CITIES OF GOLD. THE STREETS GLISTEN DAY AND NIGHT, AND THE HOMES GLITTER IN THE SUN.

THIS INFORMATION REACHED VICEROY MENDOZA FROM THE FRANCISCAN FRIAR. MENDOZA CHOSE CORONADO TO LEAD AN EXPEDITION TO FIND CÍBOLA BY LAND AND BY SEA. TO PAY FOR THE EXPEDITION, THEY PUT UP ALL THEIR WEALTH.

THEY SAY THE STREETS ARE PAVED WITH GOLD.

ACCORDING TO THE SPANIARD, THE GOLD IS THERE. IT IS UP TO YOU TO FIND IT.

WE WILL BE RICH BEYOND OUR WILDEST DREAMS.

A FLEET OF SHIPS LED BY HERNANDO DE ALARCÓN WOULD TRAVEL BY SEA TO CARRY SUPPLIES.

WE WILL SAIL UP THE COAST AND MEET CORONADO AHEAD.

CORONADO ASSEMBLED AN ARMY OF MORE THAN 1,000 MEN, INCLUDING SPANIARDS, NATIVE AMERICANS, MONKS, AND SLAVES. THEY WERE TO TRAVEL BY LAND. ON FEBRUARY 23, 1540, CORONADO SET OUT IN SEARCH OF THE SEVEN CITIES OF GOLD.

CORONADO AND HIS MEN TRAVELED OVER ROUGH **TERRAIN**, CROSSING RIVERS AND MOUNTAINS, INTO WHAT IS NOW ARIZONA.

FINALLY, IN THE LAND OF THE ZUNIS, THE SPANISH SAW A CITY ON A HILL IN THE DISTANCE.

CÍBOLA! WE FOUND IT!

WE CLAIM THIS LAND FOR SPAIN.

GO AWAY FROM HERE! YOU MAY NOT ENTER OUR VILLAGE!

BY THIS TIME, CORONADO AND HIS MEN WERE LOW ON FOOD AND FACING **STARVATION**. WHEN THEY TRIED TO ENTER THE VILLAGE OF HAWIKU, ON THE OUTSKIRTS OF CÍBOLA, THE ZUNIS TURNED THEM AWAY.

CORONADO ORDERED HIS MEN TO TAKE THE VILLAGE BY FORCE. THEY ATTACKED AND DEFEATED THE ZUNIS.

WHEN THEY ENTERED CÍBOLA, CORONADO AND HIS MEN DISCOVERED THAT IT CONSISTED ONLY OF NATIVE AMERICAN PUEBLOS WITH HOUSES MADE OF ADOBE.

THERE IS NO GOLD HERE, ONLY ADOBE HUTS.

CORONADO WAS WOUNDED DURING THE BATTLE OF CÍBOLA. WHILE HE RECOVERED, HE SENT OUT **SCOUTING PARTIES** TO CONTINUE EXPLORING THE LAND.

DÍAZ, YOU HEAD NORTH. ALVARADO, YOU HEAD EAST.

ONE GROUP, LED BY MELCHIOR DÍAZ, CAME UPON THE COLORADO RIVER.

ANOTHER GROUP, LED BY GARCÍA LÓPEZ DE CÁRDENAS, BECAME THE FIRST EUROPEANS EVER TO SEE THE GRAND CANYON.

MEANWHILE, ALARCÓN'S FLEET SAILED UP THE COLORADO RIVER. THEY COULD SEE CORONADO'S MEN BUT WERE UNABLE TO REACH THEM.

HERNANDO DE ALVARADO WAS EXPLORING THE RIO GRANDE IN WHAT IS TODAY NEW MEXICO. IN A FERTILE PLAIN, HE CAME ACROSS A NATIVE AMERICAN VILLAGE CALLED TIGUEX.

There is no gold here, but there is plenty of food.

Alvarado sent a message to Coronado about the wealth in Tiguex. Coronado, who had recovered from his wound, went there to make it his new headquarters.

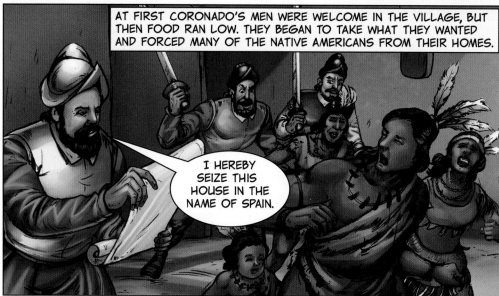

At first Coronado's men were welcome in the village, but then food ran low. They began to take what they wanted and forced many of the Native Americans from their homes.

I hereby seize this house in the name of Spain.

The Spanish let their horses and mules graze freely in the cornfields. The animals ate all the crops and destroyed the fields.

Please, leave us something to eat. We fed you, and now you will starve us.

THE NATIVE AMERICANS DECIDED TO FIGHT BACK. THEY KILLED 40 HORSES AND MULES TO SAVE THEIR CROPS.

QUIET. DO NOT WAKE ANYONE.

CORONADO'S MEN STRUCK BACK BY ATTACKING THE NATIVE AMERICANS. THIS SET OFF THE TIGUEX WAR, WHICH LASTED FOR SEVERAL MONTHS DURING 1540 AND 1541. IN A FINAL BATTLE, MOST OF THE NATIVE AMERICANS WERE KILLED.

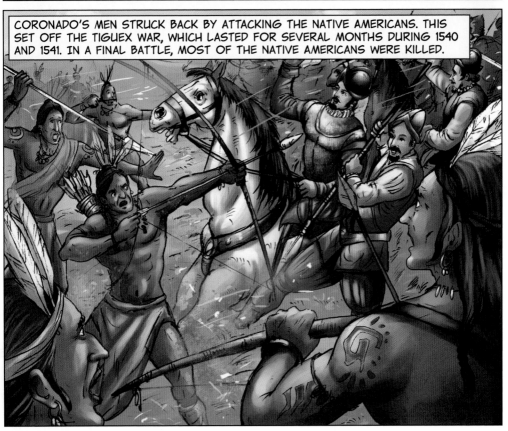

WHILE HE WAS IN TIGUEX, CORONADO WAS TOLD OF ANOTHER RICH CITY TO THE NORTH CALLED QUIVIRA. IN THE SPRING OF 1541, HE SET OFF FROM TIGUEX TO FIND IT.

QUIVIRA HAS TO BE ONE OF THE CITIES OF GOLD.

THE SPANISH CROSSED THE PECOS RIVER INTO THE REGION NOW KNOWN AS THE TEXAS PANHANDLE. THEY WERE AWED BY THE GREAT PLAINS, WHICH STRETCHED AS FAR AS THE EYE COULD SEE.

THEY SAW VAST HERDS OF BUFFALO NUMBERING IN THE THOUSANDS.

AFTER SEVERAL WEEKS, THEY MET A TRIBE OF NATIVE AMERICANS THAT CORONADO CALLED THE QUERECHOS. EXPERTS TODAY BELIEVE THE QUERECHOS WERE APACHES.

WELCOME, STRANGER.

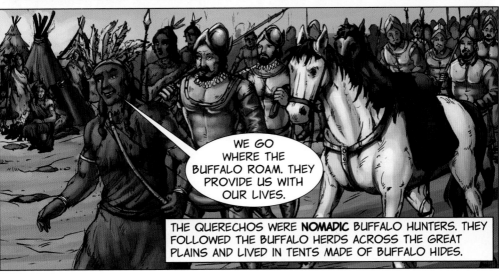

WE GO WHERE THE BUFFALO ROAM. THEY PROVIDE US WITH OUR LIVES.

THE QUERECHOS WERE **NOMADIC** BUFFALO HUNTERS. THEY FOLLOWED THE BUFFALO HERDS ACROSS THE GREAT PLAINS AND LIVED IN TENTS MADE OF BUFFALO HIDES.

CORONADO CONTINUED ON HIS **QUEST** SOUTHEAST INTO A LANDSCAPE FILLED WITH CANYONS.

IN 1541, HE MET ANOTHER TRIBE OF NATIVE AMERICANS CALLED THE TEYAS. THE TEYAS WERE THE ENEMIES OF THE QUERECHOS. THEY HUNTED BUFFALO LIKE THE QUERECHOS, BUT THEY ALSO **CULTIVATED** FRUITS AND NUTS.

CORONADO TOLD THE TEYAS HE WAS SEARCHING FOR QUIVIRA. THEY TOLD HIM HE WAS HEADED THE WRONG WAY.

YOU NEED TO HEAD THAT WAY.

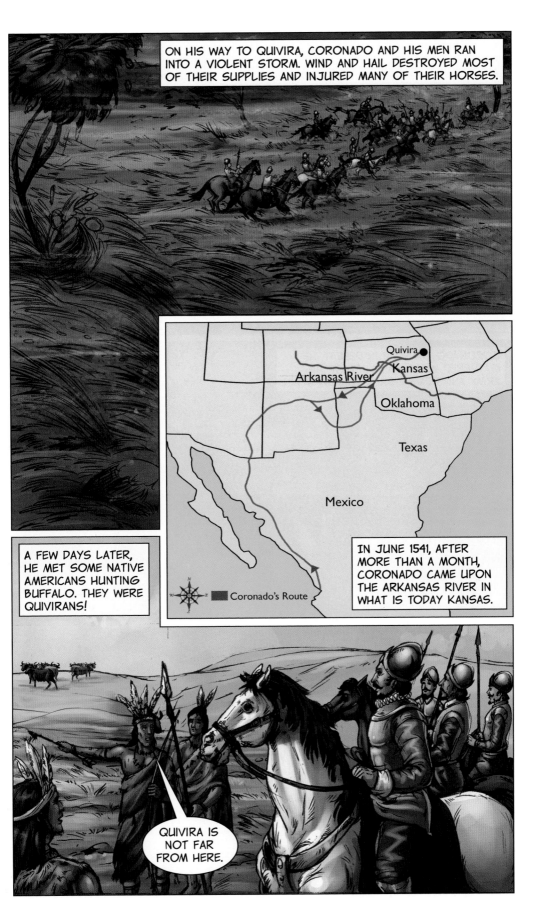

ON HIS WAY TO QUIVIRA, CORONADO AND HIS MEN RAN INTO A VIOLENT STORM. WIND AND HAIL DESTROYED MOST OF THEIR SUPPLIES AND INJURED MANY OF THEIR HORSES.

Quivira

Arkansas River

Kansas

Oklahoma

Texas

Mexico

N

W E

S

Coronado's Route

A FEW DAYS LATER, HE MET SOME NATIVE AMERICANS HUNTING BUFFALO. THEY WERE QUIVIRANS!

IN JUNE 1541, AFTER MORE THAN A MONTH, CORONADO CAME UPON THE ARKANSAS RIVER IN WHAT IS TODAY KANSAS.

QUIVIRA IS NOT FAR FROM HERE.

AFTER A JOURNEY OF THREE DAYS, CORONADO ARRIVED IN QUIVIRA. HE DISCOVERED IT WAS ONLY A POOR VILLAGE. AGAIN, THERE WAS NO GOLD.

WHAT DO YOU MEAN BY "GOLD"?

CORONADO GAVE UP IN DEFEAT. HE GATHERED WHAT WAS LEFT OF HIS ARMY AND HEADED BACK TO NEW SPAIN.

ALONG THE WAY, CORONADO SUFFERED ANOTHER SETBACK. HE WAS THROWN FROM HIS HORSE AND INJURED HIS HEAD.

HE RETURNED TO NEW SPAIN IN 1542. VICEROY MENDOZA WAS **OUTRAGED** THAT CORONADO HAD FAILED TO FIND THE SEVEN CITIES OF GOLD.

YOUR EXPEDITION HAS COST US A FORTUNE! HOW CAN YOU HAVE RETURNED WITH NOTHING!

THE SEVEN CITIES OF GOLD ARE NOTHING BUT A LEGEND, A **MYTH**. THERE WAS NOTHING TO FIND BUT POOR VILLAGES.

IN 1544, CORONADO WAS CHARGED WITH COMMITTING CRIMES AGAINST THE NATIVE AMERICANS AND REMOVED AS GOVERNOR.

WE FIND YOU GUILTY.

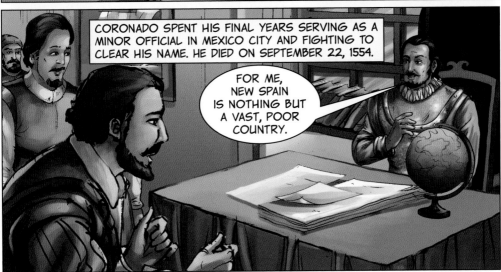

CORONADO SPENT HIS FINAL YEARS SERVING AS A MINOR OFFICIAL IN MEXICO CITY AND FIGHTING TO CLEAR HIS NAME. HE DIED ON SEPTEMBER 22, 1554.

FOR ME, NEW SPAIN IS NOTHING BUT A VAST, POOR COUNTRY.

Timeline and Map

1510 Francisco Vásquez de Coronado is born in Salamanca, Spain.

1535 Coronado travels to New Spain (Mexico) to work for Viceroy Antonio de Mendoza.

1538 Coronado is made governor of Nueva Galicia.

1539 Viceroy Mendoza appoints Coronado to lead an expedition to find Cíbola.

1540 On February 23, Coronado sets out on his expedition.

Coronado finds Cibola in modern-day Arizona, but there is no gold. He fights with Native Americans and is wounded.

Coronado splits up his forces. They discover the Colorado River, the Grand Canyon, and the village of Tiguex.

1540 –1541 Coronado fights the Tiguex War against the Native Americans of Tiguex, and most of them are killed.

1541 Coronado sets out in search of the city of Quivira. He crosses the Great Plains into modern-day Texas.

Coronado crosses the Arkansas River and finds Quivira, a poor city that has no gold, in modern-day Kansas.

1542 Coronado returns to New Spain and resumes his position as governor.

1544 Coronado is charged with committing crimes against Native Americans and removed as governor.

1554 Coronado dies in Mexico City on September 22.

Map of Francisco Vásquez de Coronado's Route

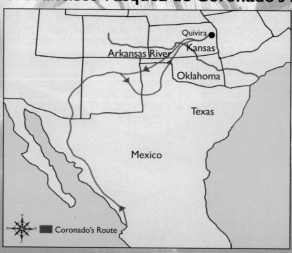

Glossary

administrators (ed-MIH-neh-stray-terz) People who direct or manage things.

appointed (uh-POYNT-ed) Named to serve in a particular position.

conquistador (kon-KEES-tuh-dor) A Spanish soldier who explored and conquered large areas of the Americas between 1500 and 1600.

cultivated (KUL-tih-vayt-ed) Grew crops for food.

expedition (ek-spuh-DIH-shun) A trip for a special purpose.

friar (FRY-ur) A brother in a communal religious order. Friars can be priests.

inherit (in-HER-it) To receive something from a parent or after the former owner dies.

legendary (LEH-jen-der-ee) Of or relating to a person who has been famous and honored for a very long time.

myth (MITH) A story that people make up to explain events.

nomadic (noh-MA-dik) Roaming about from place to place.

outraged (OWT-rayjd) Extremely angry.

quest (KWEST) A search for something important.

scouting parties (SKOWT-ing PAR-teez) People who are sent ahead to explore an area and then report back to a group leader.

starvation (star-VAY-shun) The act of suffering or dying from hunger.

terrain (tuh-RAYN) A piece of land or the physical qualities of a piece of land.

viceroy (VYS-roy) The person who runs a country for the king or the queen.

Index

Websites

Due to the changing nature of Internet links, PowerKids Press has developed an online list of websites related to the subject of this book. This site is updated regularly. Please use this link to access the list:

www.powerkidslinks.com/jgff/coro/